top + bottom + both sides (in inches)	+ 12"- 14" =	(for joining binding strips)	/40" =	round up to nearest whole number	x 2.5" =	#of binding strips needed (round up to the nearest 1/8 yard increment)

Commonly Used Quilting Terms

Bias: A fabric's direction 45 degrees to its grain. Cutting a fabric on the bias generally means it will have a little more stretch.

Connector: A small square of fabric sewn on the diagonal to create a triangle shape on a larger square or rectangle (sometimes referred to as a "stitch and flip" corner).

Foundation Piecing: A method of attaching quilt pieces by first sewing them to foundation paper. It's especially useful for complicated designs.

HST: Half-square triangle.

Piecing: Sewing pieces of fabric together to form a shape.

Quilt As You Go: A quilt-making process in which the quilt layers are assembled in pieces rather than at the end.

RSD: Right side of fabric down.

RST: Right sides of the fabrics together.

RSU: Right side of fabric up.

Sashing: Strips of fabric that go between the blocks of a quilt.

Seam Allowance: The amount of space in between stitching and the edge of the fabric.

Selvage: The finished edge of a fabric that's produced in manufacturing and gets cut off before quilting.

Stash: Collection of fabrics a quilter owns.

Strip Piecing: Sewing strips together first, then cutting them into blocks.

UFO: UnFinished Object. All those partial quilts in your closet.

WOF: Width of Fabric—selvage to selvage—usually 40" to 42" (101.6 to 106.68cm) of usable fabric.

This journal holds the works in
process and gorgeous quilts of:

If found, please contact:

Favorite Sources

Use this space to note addresses, websites, hours, and phone numbers of your favorite sources for patterns and supplies.

Quilt Groups I Belong to

_____

_____

_____

_____

_____

_____

_____

_____

_____

_____

_____

Friends are the stitches in the quilt of life.

My Longarm Quilters

_____

_____

_____

_____

_____

_____

My Quilt Appraiser

_____

_____

_____

_____

_____

_____

Wish List

Here's a place to write down the classes you dream of taking, fabrics you covet, tools you want to try someday, and whatever else is on your quilting bucket list.

Martelli's Ticket # 6206024

Works in Progress

Project	Date	Pg. No.

Quilt while you're ahead!

Project	Date	Pg. No.

Works in Progress

Project	Date	Pg. No.

Quilting fills my days...and all my closets.

Project	Date	Pg. No.

Works in Progress

Project	Date	Pg. No.

Quilt with love for those you love.

Project	Date	Pg. No.

Works in Progress

Project	Date	Pg. No.

One quilter's scrap is another quilter's treasure.

Project	Date	Pg. No.

Prepare for Class

Class Date and Time:

_____

Place:

_____

Teacher:

_____

Print a photo of the class project and cut apart.
Paste the colors from the sample project on the left, and attach
a small swatch of the fabric you are using on the right.

Class Sample Fabric
(Description)

My Fabrics

Finished Project

Construction Notes

_____

_____

_____

_____

_____

_____

_____

_____

_____

_____

Prepare for Class

Class Date and Time:

_____

Place:

_____

Teacher:

_____

Print a photo of the class project and cut apart.
Paste the colors from the sample project on the left, and attach
a small swatch of the fabric you are using on the right.

Class Sample Fabric
(Description)

My Fabrics

Finished Project

Construction Notes

_____

_____

_____

_____

_____

_____

_____

_____

_____

_____

Prepare for Class

Class Date and Time:

_____

Place:

_____

Teacher:

_____

Print a photo of the class project and cut apart.
Paste the colors from the sample project on the left, and attach
a small swatch of the fabric you are using on the right.

Class Sample Fabric
(Description)

My Fabrics

Finished Project

Construction Notes

_____

_____

_____

_____

_____

_____

_____

_____

_____

_____

Prepare for Class

Class Date and Time:

_____

Place:

_____

Teacher:

_____

Print a photo of the class project and cut apart.
Paste the colors from the sample project on the left, and attach
a small swatch of the fabric you are using on the right.

Class Sample Fabric
(Description)

My Fabrics

Finished Project

Construction Notes

Prepare for Class

Class Date and Time:

_____

Place:

_____

Teacher:

_____

Print a photo of the class project and cut apart.
Paste the colors from the sample project on the left, and attach
a small swatch of the fabric you are using on the right.

Class Sample Fabric
(Description)

My Fabrics

Finished Project

Construction Notes

_____

_____

_____

_____

_____

_____

_____

_____

_____

_____

Pattern

_____

_____

_____

Start Date / End Date	Source
_____	_____
_____	_____
Size	**Made For**
_____	_____
_____	_____
Quilted By	**Batting Used**
_____	_____
_____	_____
Thread Used	**Quilting Design Used**
_____	_____
_____	_____
Appraisal	**Class Taken**
_____	_____
_____	_____

Special Tools

_____

_____

Finished Project

Construction Notes

_____

_____

_____

_____

_____

Fabrics Used (Notes and Swatches)

_____

_____

_____

_____

_____

Pattern

_____

_____

_____

Start Date / End Date	Source

Size	Made For

Quilted By	Batting Used

Thread Used	Quilting Design Used

Appraisal	Class Taken

Special Tools

_____

_____

Finished Project

Construction Notes

_____

_____

_____

_____

_____

Fabrics Used (Notes and Swatches)

_____

_____

_____

_____

_____

Pattern

Start Date / End Date	Source

Size	Made For

Quilted By	Batting Used

Thread Used	Quilting Design Used

Appraisal	Class Taken

Special Tools

Finished Project

Construction Notes

_____

_____

_____

_____

_____

Fabrics Used (Notes and Swatches)

_____

_____

_____

_____

_____

Pattern

_____

_____

Start Date / End Date

_____

Size

_____

Quilted By

_____

Thread Used

_____

Appraisal

_____

Source

_____

Made For

_____

Batting Used

_____

Quilting Design Used

_____

Class Taken

_____

Special Tools

_____

_____

Finished Project

Construction Notes

_____

_____

_____

_____

_____

Fabrics Used (Notes and Swatches)

_____

_____

_____

_____

_____

Pattern

_____

_____

_____

Start Date / End Date	Source

Size	Made For

Quilted By	Batting Used

Thread Used	Quilting Design Used

Appraisal	Class Taken

Special Tools

_____

_____

Finished Project

Construction Notes

_____

_____

_____

_____

_____

Fabrics Used (Notes and Swatches)

_____

_____

_____

_____

_____

Pattern

Start Date / End Date

Source

Size

Made For

Quilted By

Batting Used

Thread Used

Quilting Design Used

Appraisal

Class Taken

Special Tools

Finished Project

Construction Notes

_____

_____

_____

_____

_____

Fabrics Used (Notes and Swatches)

_____

_____

_____

_____

_____

Pattern

_____

_____

Start Date / End Date	Source
Size	**Made For**
Quilted By	**Batting Used**
Thread Used	**Quilting Design Used**
Appraisal	**Class Taken**

Special Tools

_____

_____

Finished Project

Construction Notes

_____

_____

_____

_____

_____

Fabrics Used (Notes and Swatches)

_____

_____

_____

_____

_____

Pattern

_____

_____

Start Date / End Date

_____

Source

_____

Size

_____

Made For

_____

Quilted By

_____

Batting Used

_____

Thread Used

_____

Quilting Design Used

_____

Appraisal

_____

Class Taken

_____

Special Tools

_____

_____

Finished Project

Construction Notes

_____

_____

_____

_____

_____

Fabrics Used (Notes and Swatches)

_____

_____

_____

_____

_____

Pattern

_____

_____

_____

Start Date / End Date	Source

Size	Made For

Quilted By	Batting Used

Thread Used	Quilting Design Used

Appraisal	Class Taken

Special Tools

_____

_____

Finished Project

Construction Notes

_____

_____

_____

_____

_____

Fabrics Used (Notes and Swatches)

_____

_____

_____

_____

_____

Pattern

Start Date / End Date

Source

Size

Made For

Quilted By

Batting Used

Thread Used

Quilting Design Used

Appraisal

Class Taken

Special Tools

Finished Project

Construction Notes

_____

_____

_____

_____

_____

Fabrics Used (Notes and Swatches)

_____

_____

_____

_____

_____

Pattern

_____

_____

Start Date / End Date	Source
Size	Made For
Quilted By	Batting Used
Thread Used	Quilting Design Used
Appraisal	Class Taken

Special Tools

_____

_____

Finished Project

Construction Notes

_____

_____

_____

_____

_____

Fabrics Used (Notes and Swatches)

_____

_____

_____

_____

_____

Pattern

_____

_____

_____

Start Date / End Date	**Source**

_____

Size	**Made For**

_____

Quilted By	**Batting Used**

_____

Thread Used	**Quilting Design Used**

_____

Appraisal	**Class Taken**

_____

Special Tools

_____

_____

Finished Project

Construction Notes

_____

_____

_____

_____

_____

Fabrics Used (Notes and Swatches)

_____

_____

_____

_____

_____

Pattern

_____

_____

Start Date / End Date

_____

_____

Size

_____

_____

Quilted By

_____

_____

Thread Used

_____

_____

Appraisal

_____

_____

Source

_____

_____

Made For

_____

_____

Batting Used

_____

_____

Quilting Design Used

_____

_____

Class Taken

_____

_____

Special Tools

_____

_____

Finished Project

Construction Notes

_____

_____

_____

_____

_____

Fabrics Used (Notes and Swatches)

_____

_____

_____

_____

_____

Pattern

_____

_____

Start Date / End Date

_____

_____

Source

_____

_____

Size

_____

_____

Made For

_____

_____

Quilted By

_____

_____

Batting Used

_____

_____

Thread Used

_____

_____

Quilting Design Used

_____

_____

Appraisal

_____

_____

Class Taken

_____

_____

Special Tools

_____

_____

Finished Project

Construction Notes

_____

_____

_____

_____

_____

Fabrics Used (Notes and Swatches)

_____

_____

_____

_____

_____

Pattern

_____

_____

_____

Start Date / End Date

_____

_____

Size

_____

_____

Quilted By

_____

_____

Thread Used

_____

_____

Appraisal

_____

_____

Source

_____

_____

Made For

_____

_____

Batting Used

_____

_____

Quilting Design Used

_____

_____

Class Taken

_____

_____

Special Tools

_____

_____

Finished Project

Construction Notes

_____

_____

_____

_____

_____

Fabrics Used (Notes and Swatches)

_____

_____

_____

_____

Pattern

_____

_____

_____

Start Date / End Date	Source
_____	_____

Size	Made For
_____	_____

Quilted By	Batting Used
_____	_____

Thread Used	Quilting Design Used
_____	_____

Appraisal	Class Taken
_____	_____

Special Tools

_____

_____

Finished Project

Construction Notes

_____

_____

_____

_____

_____

Fabrics Used (Notes and Swatches)

_____

_____

_____

_____

_____

Pattern

_____

_____

Start Date / End Date

_____

_____

Size

_____

_____

Quilted By

_____

_____

Thread Used

_____

_____

Appraisal

_____

_____

Source

_____

_____

Made For

_____

_____

Batting Used

_____

_____

Quilting Design Used

_____

_____

Class Taken

_____

_____

Special Tools

_____

_____

Finished Project

Construction Notes

_____

_____

_____

_____

_____

Fabrics Used (Notes and Swatches)

_____

_____

_____

_____

_____

Pattern

_____

_____

_____

Start Date / End Date

_____

_____

Source

_____

_____

Size

_____

_____

Made For

_____

_____

Quilted By

_____

_____

Batting Used

_____

_____

Thread Used

_____

_____

Quilting Design Used

_____

_____

Appraisal

_____

_____

Class Taken

_____

_____

Special Tools

_____

_____

Finished Project

Construction Notes

_____

_____

_____

_____

_____

Fabrics Used (Notes and Swatches)

_____

_____

_____

_____

_____

Pattern

_____

_____

_____

Start Date / End Date	Source

Size	Made For

Quilted By	Batting Used

Thread Used	Quilting Design Used

Appraisal	Class Taken

Special Tools

_____

_____

Finished Project

Construction Notes

_____

_____

_____

_____

_____

Fabrics Used (Notes and Swatches)

_____

_____

_____

_____

_____

Pattern

_____

_____

_____

Start Date / End Date

Source

_____

Size

Made For

_____

Quilted By

Batting Used

_____

Thread Used

Quilting Design Used

_____

Appraisal

Class Taken

_____

Special Tools

_____

_____

Finished Project

Construction Notes

_____

_____

_____

_____

_____

Fabrics Used (Notes and Swatches)

_____

_____

_____

_____

_____

Pattern

_____

_____

Start Date / End Date

_____

_____

Source

_____

_____

Size

_____

_____

Made For

_____

_____

Quilted By

_____

_____

Batting Used

_____

_____

Thread Used

_____

_____

Quilting Design Used

_____

_____

Appraisal

_____

_____

Class Taken

_____

_____

Special Tools

_____

_____

Finished Project

Construction Notes

_____

_____

_____

_____

_____

Fabrics Used (Notes and Swatches)

_____

_____

_____

_____

_____

Pattern

_____

_____

_____

Start Date / End Date	**Source**
Size	**Made For**
Quilted By	**Batting Used**
Thread Used	**Quilting Design Used**
Appraisal	**Class Taken**

Special Tools

_____

_____

Finished Project

Construction Notes

_____

_____

_____

_____

_____

Fabrics Used (Notes and Swatches)

_____

_____

_____

_____

_____

Pattern

_____

_____

_____

Start Date / End Date

_____

Source

_____

Size

_____

Made For

_____

Quilted By

_____

Batting Used

_____

Thread Used

_____

Quilting Design Used

_____

Appraisal

_____

Class Taken

_____

Special Tools

_____

_____

Finished Project

Construction Notes

_____

_____

_____

_____

_____

Fabrics Used (Notes and Swatches)

_____

_____

_____

_____

_____

Pattern

_____

_____

_____

Start Date / End Date

Source

_____

_____

Size

Made For

_____

_____

Quilted By

Batting Used

_____

_____

Thread Used

Quilting Design Used

_____

_____

Appraisal

Class Taken

_____

_____

Special Tools

_____

_____

Finished Project

Construction Notes

_____

_____

_____

_____

_____

Fabrics Used (Notes and Swatches)

_____

_____

_____

_____

_____

Pattern

Start Date / End Date

Source

Size

Made For

Quilted By

Batting Used

Thread Used

Quilting Design Used

Appraisal

Class Taken

Special Tools

Finished Project

Construction Notes

_____

_____

_____

_____

_____

Fabrics Used (Notes and Swatches)

_____

_____

_____

_____

_____

Pattern

_____

_____

_____

Start Date / End Date	Source

_____

Size	Made For

_____

Quilted By	Batting Used

_____

Thread Used	Quilting Design Used

_____

Appraisal	Class Taken

_____

Special Tools

_____

_____

Finished Project

Construction Notes

_____

_____

_____

_____

_____

Fabrics Used (Notes and Swatches)

_____

_____

_____

_____

_____

Pattern

_____

_____

_____

Start Date / End Date

Source

_____

_____

Size

Made For

_____

_____

Quilted By

Batting Used

_____

_____

Thread Used

Quilting Design Used

_____

_____

Appraisal

Class Taken

_____

_____

Special Tools

_____

_____

Finished Project

Construction Notes

_____

_____

_____

_____

_____

Fabrics Used (Notes and Swatches)

_____

_____

_____

_____

_____

Pattern

_____

_____

_____

Start Date / End Date

_____

_____

Source

_____

_____

Size

_____

_____

Made For

_____

_____

Quilted By

_____

_____

Batting Used

_____

_____

Thread Used

_____

_____

Quilting Design Used

_____

_____

Appraisal

_____

_____

Class Taken

_____

_____

Special Tools

_____

_____

Finished Project

Construction Notes

_____

_____

_____

_____

_____

Fabrics Used (Notes and Swatches)

_____

_____

_____

_____

_____

Pattern

_____

_____

_____

Start Date / End Date	Source

Size	Made For

Quilted By	Batting Used

Thread Used	Quilting Design Used

Appraisal	Class Taken

Special Tools

_____

_____

Finished Project

Construction Notes

_____

_____

_____

_____

_____

Fabrics Used (Notes and Swatches)

_____

_____

_____

_____

_____

Pattern

_____

_____

_____

Start Date / End Date	Source
Size	**Made For**
Quilted By	**Batting Used**
Thread Used	**Quilting Design Used**
Appraisal	**Class Taken**

Special Tools

_____

_____

Finished Project

Construction Notes

_____

_____

_____

_____

_____

Fabrics Used (Notes and Swatches)

_____

_____

_____

_____

_____

Pattern

_____

_____

_____

Start Date / End Date	Source
_____	_____
_____	_____
Size	**Made For**
_____	_____
_____	_____
Quilted By	**Batting Used**
_____	_____
_____	_____
Thread Used	**Quilting Design Used**
_____	_____
_____	_____
Appraisal	**Class Taken**
_____	_____
_____	_____

Special Tools

_____

_____

Finished Project

Construction Notes

_____

_____

_____

_____

_____

Fabrics Used (Notes and Swatches)

_____

_____

_____

_____

_____

Pattern

_____

_____

_____

Start Date / End Date	**Source**

_____

Size	**Made For**

_____

Quilted By	**Batting Used**

_____

Thread Used	**Quilting Design Used**

_____

Appraisal	**Class Taken**

_____

Special Tools

_____

_____

Finished Project

Construction Notes

_____

_____

_____

_____

_____

Fabrics Used (Notes and Swatches)

_____

_____

_____

_____

_____

Pattern

_____

_____

Start Date / End Date	Source

Size	Made For

Quilted By	Batting Used

Thread Used	Quilting Design Used

Appraisal	Class Taken

Special Tools

_____

_____

Finished Project

Construction Notes

_____

_____

_____

_____

_____

Fabrics Used (Notes and Swatches)

_____

_____

_____

_____

_____

Pattern

_____

_____

_____

Start Date / End Date	Source

_____

Size	Made For

_____

Quilted By	Batting Used

_____

Thread Used	Quilting Design Used

_____

Appraisal	Class Taken

_____

Special Tools

_____

_____

Finished Project

Construction Notes

_____

_____

_____

_____

_____

Fabrics Used (Notes and Swatches)

_____

_____

_____

_____

_____

Pattern

_____

_____

_____

Start Date / End Date	Source

Size	Made For

Quilted By	Batting Used

Thread Used	Quilting Design Used

Appraisal	Class Taken

Special Tools

_____

_____

Finished Project

Construction Notes

_____

_____

_____

_____

_____

Fabrics Used (Notes and Swatches)

_____

_____

_____

_____

_____

Pattern

_____

_____

_____

Start Date / End Date	Source
_____	_____
_____	_____

Size	Made For
_____	_____
_____	_____

Quilted By	Batting Used
_____	_____
_____	_____

Thread Used	Quilting Design Used
_____	_____
_____	_____

Appraisal	Class Taken
_____	_____
_____	_____

Special Tools

_____

_____

Finished Project

Construction Notes

_____

_____

_____

_____

_____

Fabrics Used (Notes and Swatches)

_____

_____

_____

_____

_____

Pattern

Start Date / End Date

Source

Size

Made For

Quilted By

Batting Used

Thread Used

Quilting Design Used

Appraisal

Class Taken

Special Tools

Finished Project

Construction Notes

_____

_____

_____

_____

_____

Fabrics Used (Notes and Swatches)

_____

_____

_____

_____

_____

Pattern

_____

_____

Start Date / End Date

_____

_____

Source

_____

_____

Size

_____

_____

Made For

_____

_____

Quilted By

_____

_____

Batting Used

_____

_____

Thread Used

_____

_____

Quilting Design Used

_____

_____

Appraisal

_____

_____

Class Taken

_____

_____

Special Tools

_____

_____

Finished Project

Construction Notes

_____

_____

_____

_____

_____

Fabrics Used (Notes and Swatches)

_____

_____

_____

_____

_____

Pattern

_____

_____

_____

Start Date / End Date

_____

_____

Size

_____

_____

Quilted By

_____

_____

Thread Used

_____

_____

Appraisal

_____

_____

Source

_____

_____

Made For

_____

_____

Batting Used

_____

_____

Quilting Design Used

_____

_____

Class Taken

_____

_____

Special Tools

_____

_____

Finished Project

Construction Notes

_____

_____

_____

_____

_____

Fabrics Used (Notes and Swatches)

_____

_____

_____

_____

_____

Pattern

_____

_____

Start Date / End Date	**Source**

Size	**Made For**

Quilted By	**Batting Used**

Thread Used	**Quilting Design Used**

Appraisal	**Class Taken**

Special Tools

_____

_____

Finished Project

Construction Notes

_____

_____

_____

_____

_____

Fabrics Used (Notes and Swatches)

_____

_____

_____

_____

_____

Pattern

_____

_____

Start Date / End Date	Source

Size	Made For

Quilted By	Batting Used

Thread Used	Quilting Design Used

Appraisal	Class Taken

Special Tools

_____

_____

Finished Project

Construction Notes

_____

_____

_____

_____

_____

Fabrics Used (Notes and Swatches)

_____

_____

_____

_____

_____

Pattern

_____

_____

_____

Start Date / End Date	Source

Size	Made For

Quilted By	Batting Used

Thread Used	Quilting Design Used

Appraisal	Class Taken

Special Tools

_____

_____

Finished Project

Construction Notes

_____

_____

_____

_____

_____

Fabrics Used (Notes and Swatches)

_____

_____

_____

_____

_____

Pattern

_____

_____

Start Date / End Date

_____

Size

_____

Quilted By

_____

Thread Used

_____

Appraisal

_____

Source

_____

Made For

_____

Batting Used

_____

Quilting Design Used

_____

Class Taken

_____

Special Tools

_____

_____

Finished Project

Construction Notes

_____

_____

_____

_____

Fabrics Used (Notes and Swatches)

_____

_____

_____

_____

_____

Pattern

Start Date / End Date

Source

Size

Made For

Quilted By

Batting Used

Thread Used

Quilting Design Used

Appraisal

Class Taken

Special Tools

Finished Project

Construction Notes

_____

_____

_____

_____

_____

Fabrics Used (Notes and Swatches)

_____

_____

_____

_____

_____

Pattern

_____

_____

Start Date / End Date

_____

_____

Source

_____

_____

Size

_____

_____

Made For

_____

_____

Quilted By

_____

_____

Batting Used

_____

_____

Thread Used

_____

_____

Quilting Design Used

_____

_____

Appraisal

_____

_____

Class Taken

_____

_____

Special Tools

_____

_____

Finished Project

Construction Notes

_____

_____

_____

_____

_____

Fabrics Used (Notes and Swatches)

_____

_____

_____

_____

_____

Pattern

_____

_____

_____

Start Date / End Date	Source

_____

_____

Size	Made For

_____

_____

Quilted By	Batting Used

_____

_____

Thread Used	Quilting Design Used

_____

_____

Appraisal	Class Taken

_____

_____

Special Tools

_____

_____

Finished Project

Construction Notes

_____

_____

_____

_____

_____

Fabrics Used (Notes and Swatches)

_____

_____

_____

_____

_____

Pattern

_____

_____

_____

Start Date / End Date	**Source**
Size	**Made For**
Quilted By	**Batting Used**
Thread Used	**Quilting Design Used**
Appraisal	**Class Taken**

Special Tools

_____

_____

Finished Project

Construction Notes

_____

_____

_____

_____

_____

Fabrics Used (Notes and Swatches)

_____

_____

_____

_____

_____

Pattern

_____

_____

_____

Start Date / End Date	Source
_____	_____
_____	_____

Size	Made For
_____	_____
_____	_____

Quilted By	Batting Used
_____	_____
_____	_____

Thread Used	Quilting Design Used
_____	_____
_____	_____

Appraisal	Class Taken
_____	_____
_____	_____

Special Tools

_____

_____

Finished Project

Construction Notes

_____

_____

_____

_____

_____

Fabrics Used (Notes and Swatches)

_____

_____

_____

_____

_____

Pattern

Start Date / End Date

Source

Size

Made For

Quilted By

Batting Used

Thread Used

Quilting Design Used

Appraisal

Class Taken

Special Tools

Finished Project

Construction Notes

_____

_____

_____

_____

_____

Fabrics Used (Notes and Swatches)

_____

_____

_____

_____

_____

Pattern

_____
_____
_____

Start Date / End Date

_____
_____

Source

_____
_____

Size

_____
_____

Made For

_____
_____

Quilted By

_____
_____

Batting Used

_____
_____

Thread Used

_____
_____

Quilting Design Used

_____
_____

Appraisal

_____
_____

Class Taken

_____
_____

Special Tools

_____
_____

Finished Project

Construction Notes

_____

_____

_____

_____

_____

Fabrics Used (Notes and Swatches)

_____

_____

_____

_____

_____

About the Author

Linda J. Hahn is the author of six books and has won several awards for them. Her book *New York Beauty Simplified*, a bronze medal winner in the Independent Publishers Living Now Book Awards, is a best-seller. The follow-up book, *New York Beauty Diversified* (AQS 2013), was the gold medal winner in 2013. She has four additional books: *Rock That Quilt Block — Weathervane* (AQS 2015), *Rock That Quilt Block — Hourglass* (AQS 2016), *Quilt Match Up — Cash Vs. Stash* (AQS 2016), and *New York Beauty Quilts Electrified* (Landauer Publishing 2019).

Linda is the designer of the Island Vibes fabric collection by Banyan Batiks for Northcott. She also has a coordinating thread collection with Aurifil.

ISBN 978-1-64178-096-4

Fox Chapel Publishing makes every effort to use environmentally friendly paper for printing.

We are always looking for talented authors and artists. To submit an idea, please send a brief inquiry to acquisitions@foxchapelpublishing.com.

Printed in Malaysia
First printing

How Many Squares Will I Get?

SQUARE SIZE	FABRIC YARDAGE							
	¼ yard	½ yard	¾ yard	1 yard	1 ¼ yards	1 ½ yards	1 ¾ yards	2 yards
2"	80	180	260	360	440	540	620	720
2 ½"	48	112	160	224	288	336	400	448
3"	39	78	117	156	195	236	273	312
3 ½"	22	44	77	110	132	165	198	220
4"	20	40	60	90	110	130	150	180
4 ½"	18	36	54	72	90	108	126	144
5"	8	24	40	56	72	80	96	112
5 ½"	7	21	28	42	56	63	77	91
6"	6	18	24	36	42	54	60	72
6 ½"	6	12	24	30	36	48	54	66
7"	5	10	15	25	30	35	45	60
7 ½"	5	10	15	20	30	35	40	45
8"	5	10	15	20	25	30	35	45
8 ½"	4	8	12	16	20	24	28	32
9"	4	8	12	16	20	24	28	32
9 ½"	n/a	4	8	12	16	20	24	28
10"	n/a	4	8	12	16	20	24	28
10 ½"	n/a	3	6	9	12	18	15	18
11"	n/a	3	6	9	12	12	15	18
11 ½"	n/a	3	6	9	9	12	15	18
12"	n/a	3	6	9	9	12	15	18